SPORTS
DYNASTIES

D1066586

MICHAEL JORDAN
AND THE CHICAGO BULLS

BY TYLER MASON

SportsZone

An Imprint of Abdo Publishing
abdopublishing.com

abdopublishing.com

Published by Abdo Publishing, a division of ABDO, PO Box 398166, Minneapolis, Minnesota 55439.

Printed in the United States of America, North Mankato, Minnesota
042018
092018

THIS BOOK CONTAINS
RECYCLED MATERIALS

Distributed in paperback by North Star Editions, Inc.

Cover Photos: John Swart/AP Images, left; Al Messerschmidt/AP Images, right
Interior Photos: John Biever/Icon Sportswire/Getty Images, 4–5; John Biever/Sports Illustrated/Getty
Images, 6, 42; Mark J. Terill/AP Images, 9, 20–21, 26; Beth A. Keiser/AP Images, 10, 23; Fred Jewell/AP
Images, 12–13, 24; Robert Willett/AP Images, 14; Focus On Sport/Getty Images Sport/Getty Images, 17;
John Swart/AP Images, 18; Jon Sall/AP Images, 28–29; Richard Mackson/Sports Illustrated/Getty Images,
30; Dave Martin/AP Images, 32; Jack Smith/AP Images, 35; Michael Conroy/AP Images, 36–37; Jeff Siner/
Charlotte Observer/MCT/Newscom, 38; Zara Vila/Shutterstock Images, 41

Editor: Bradley Cole
Series Designer: Craig Hinton

Library of Congress Control Number: 2017962587

Publisher's Cataloging-in-Publication Data

Names: Mason, Tyler, author.
Title: Michael Jordan and the Chicago Bulls / by Tyler Mason.
Description: Minneapolis, Minnesota : Abdo Publishing, 2019. | Series: Sports dynasties | Includes online
     resources and index.
Identifiers: ISBN 9781532114342 (lib.bdg.) | ISBN 9781641852838 (pbk) | ISBN 9781532154171 (ebook)
Subjects: LCSH: Jordan, Michael, 1963-.--Juvenile literature. | Basketball players--United States--
     Biography--Juvenile literature. | Basketball--Juvenile literature. | Chicago Bulls (Basketball
     team)--Juvenile literature.
Classification: DDC 796.323092 [B]--dc23

TABLE OF
CONTENTS

CHAPTER 1

GAME WINNER

There was no doubt who would take the final shot. The Chicago Bulls had already won five National Basketball Association (NBA) championships. Michael Jordan was the NBA Finals Most Valuable Player (MVP) on all of those teams. He was the face of the franchise, and there were whispers that this might be his last game.

On June 14, 1998, Jordan and the Bulls were one win away from their sixth title. After losing

Michael Jordan and the Chicago Bulls were down but not out at the end of Game 6 of the 1998 NBA Finals.

the first game of the Finals, Chicago had beaten the Utah Jazz in the next three games. Utah won Game 5. That meant the Bulls led the series 3–2 heading into Game 6.

It was a thrilling game played in front of Utah's rowdy home crowd. Chicago trailed by one point with 18.9 seconds to play. The Jazz had the ball, but Jordan stole it from Utah star forward Karl Malone and raced toward the other end of the court to set up the Bulls' final shot.

Utah's Byron Russell guarded Jordan on the final play. Jordan drove hard to his right, and Russell reached for the ball. Jordan pulled a crossover to create open space for a shot. With Russell stumbling, Jordan had a clear look at the basket. His 20-foot jump shot was good. He kept his hand in the air after the ball went through the basket. That pose is one of the most iconic images in NBA history.

The basket gave Chicago an 87–86 lead with 5.2 seconds to play. Utah's John Stockton missed a last-ditch three-point shot. The Bulls had won their sixth NBA title in eight years. It was the second time Chicago had won three championships in a row. This was also the second year in a row the Bulls beat the Jazz in the Finals. And they joined the Los Angeles Lakers and Boston Celtics as the only teams to win at least six NBA titles.

Jordan was clutch late in Game 6. He scored 16 points in the fourth quarter, including the final eight Chicago points to carry the Bulls to victory. Jordan was named the NBA Finals MVP for the sixth time in his career. He averaged 33.5 points per game during the series against Utah. Of course, Jordan saved his best for last.

THE SHOT

Michael Jordan's famous shot in Game 6 in 1998 was not his only game-winning shot in the playoffs. Another of his well-known game-winners is known as "the Shot." Jordan hit a buzzer-beater against the Cleveland Cavaliers in Game 5 of the first round of the 1989 NBA playoffs. That shot gave Chicago a 101–100 win to advance to the second round.

But Jordan didn't do it alone. He had a talented supporting cast during the 1997–98 season. Forwards Scottie Pippen and

The Bulls roster that won their second three-peat would disband after the 1998 season.

Toni Kukoč made big plays to help Chicago win games earlier in the series. Dennis Rodman was an important piece on defense and a rebounding machine. Point guard Ron Harper started all

21 games that postseason. While Jordan was the hero, the title was a team effort.

JORDAN'S LAST SHOT

Jordan finished his final game as a Bull with 45 points. He scored more than half of his team's points that night. No shot Jordan took that game was bigger than his last one. It also turned out to be the last shot he ever took for the Bulls. Jordan retired after 13 seasons with Chicago.

The Chicago Bulls dynasty had plenty of great moments. Jordan was responsible for many of them. But that Game 6 victory on June 14, 1998, marked the end of the Bulls as a basketball dynasty. Jordan never played for Chicago again. Pippen was traded to the Houston Rockets the following season. Jackson left to coach the Los Angeles Lakers. The other players went their separate ways. The Bulls would never be the same. But the 1998 NBA Finals lives on as one of the top moments for the dynasty.

CHAPTER 2

ORIGIN

The Chicago Bulls dynasty of the 1990s wasn't built in a season. It took time to put together one of the best NBA teams ever. Lots of pieces had to fall into place before the organization was on its way to winning championships.

The Bulls weren't very good in the 1983–84 season. They finished just 27–55 that year. Because of that, Chicago had a high draft pick in the 1984 NBA Draft.

The Bulls were manhandled throughout the 1983–84 season, setting up their good fortune in the 1984 NBA Draft.

Jordan starred at the University of North Carolina for three years.

Only two teams got to draft before the Bulls in 1984, the Houston Rockets and Portland Trail Blazers. Houston took Hakeem Olajuwon as the first overall pick. Olajuwon was a star center at the University of Houston. Portland drafted second. The Trail Blazers also needed a center, so they chose Sam Bowie from the University of Kentucky. Two picks in and Jordan was still available.

That gave the Bulls the chance to draft the player who would go on to become the best of his generation. Chicago selected Jordan out of the University of North Carolina.

Jordan played three seasons at North Carolina. He averaged 17.7 points per game with the Tar Heels. He helped North Carolina win the national championship during his freshman season. In a sign of things to come, Jordan hit the game-winning jump shot with 17 seconds left in the title game against Georgetown. Then, as a junior in 1984, Jordan was named the Associated Press Player of the Year. He was ready for the next step.

GETTING JORDAN SOME HELP

Jordan's college success continued in the pros. The Bulls made the playoffs the very next season. It was the first of 14 straight seasons Chicago would make the playoffs. He was named the NBA Rookie of the Year during the 1984–85 season. He led the NBA in scoring for seven straight seasons, beginning with the 1986–87 season. Jordan was also an All-Star in every full season he played with the Bulls. He played in 14 All-Star Games and was the MVP of the NBA Finals each of the six times Chicago won the championship. And he went on to be the league MVP five times starting in 1988. He couldn't do everything on his own though. Chicago got him some help in 1987 when it acquired University of Central Arkansas forward Scottie Pippen. The Seattle SuperSonics drafted Pippen fifth overall and then traded him to the Bulls on draft night.

Adding Pippen was a big key for the Bulls. He had averaged 23.6 points and 10 rebounds per game his senior year at Central Arkansas. But the Bulls still needed a few more pieces before they would win a championship. One of those missing pieces was a head coach.

The Bulls cycled through three different head coaches in Jordan's first five seasons. In his rookie season they lost in the first round of the playoffs and fired coach Kevin Loughery. The next year they had the same result and fired coach Stan Albeck. Finally Doug Collins led the Bulls to a breakthrough in the playoffs. In 1988 they won their first playoff series in the Jordan era before losing to the Detroit Pistons in the

Phil Jackson took his first head coaching position with the Chicago Bulls in 1989.

Eastern Conference semifinals. The next year, they won two playoff series, but the Bulls lost to the Pistons again, this time in the conference finals.

That was it for Collins. The Bulls hired Phil Jackson to take over as the new head coach. Jackson played 10 seasons with the New York Knicks and had been a Bulls assistant the previous two seasons before he was tasked with getting Jordan and the Bulls over the hump.

In Jackson's first year as head coach, Chicago improved by eight wins, posting a record of 55–27. But once again, the Detroit Pistons stood in their way in the conference finals. In a grueling seven-game series, the Pistons sent the Bulls home without a championship ring.

At that point, it would've been fair to wonder if Jordan and the Bulls would ever put it all together and make a championship run. Little did anyone know what the guys from Chicago had in store for the NBA in the 1990s.

GENERAL MANAGER JERRY KRAUSE

Behind the scenes making all the moves to put together a championship team was Jerry Krause. He was Chicago's general manager during the Bulls dynasty. He was hired to run the team in 1985. Chicago already had Jordan on the roster. But Krause made many of the trades and draft decisions to put a championship team together.

Krause helped make the draft-night trade that landed Pippen. He also drafted several other players that would play big roles in the Bulls dynasty. He was twice named NBA Executive of the Year for his work putting together Chicago's rosters.

CHAPTER 3

SUPPORTING CAST

Jordan was the best player on each of Chicago's six championship teams, but it takes an entire team to win a championship. It also takes a great coach. There were many key figures during the Chicago Bulls dynasty. None was bigger than Michael Jordan, but each was important.

EARLY EDITIONS

Scottie Pippen was Jordan's sidekick during the two three-peats of Chicago's dynasty.

Jordan turned in a great performance during his last game as a Chicago Bull to win his sixth NBA Championship.

He was the team's second-leading scorer in all six of the Bulls' championship seasons and the team's leader when Jordan stepped away from basketball to play baseball. Pippen averaged 17.7 points per game in 12 seasons with Chicago and was selected to the All-Defensive Team 10 times.

Head coach Phil Jackson was also important in building the Bulls dynasty. Chicago was Jackson's first NBA head coaching job of his career. He used what he called the "triangle offense" in Chicago. Three players form a triangle on the court. The other two spread the defense out in the lane and on the perimeter. There are no set plays. The players running the offense are supposed to read what the defense is doing and react to it.

After Jackson took over in the 1989–90 season, the Bulls posted nine straight winning seasons. Jackson finished with a 545–193 record as Chicago's head coach and won six NBA titles. He also won the NBA Coach of the Year Award in 1996.

Horace Grant was drafted the same year as Pippen. Chicago took Grant with the 10th overall pick in 1987. He was a big piece of the Bulls' first three championships. The 6-foot-10 Grant averaged a double-double of 14.2 points and 10.0 rebounds per game during the 1991–92 season. Grant was one of the Bulls'

Head coach Phil Jackson maximized the talent on the roster and didn't have a losing season in Chicago.

leading scorers in the playoffs when they won three straight titles. He played for Chicago through 1994 before joining the Orlando Magic as a free agent the next season.

Grant was known for the goggles that he wore when he played. He originally wore them because he was legally blind. But Grant kept wearing them after having surgery on his eyes to make kids who had to wear them feel better.

LATER EDITIONS

Toni Kukoč was a lanky shooting forward from Croatia. He joined the Bulls after they won their first three titles. Kukoč was originally drafted by Chicago in the second round of the 1990 draft. He stayed in Europe for three more years, however, and didn't play for the Bulls until the 1993–94 season, when he was 25 years old.

Kukoč played against Jordan and Pippen in the 1992 Olympics. The two Bulls stars won the gold medal for the United States with the Dream Team. Kukoč played for his native Croatia in the Olympics and lost to Team USA in the gold medal game. Kukoč went on to win three championships in Chicago. He averaged double figures in scoring each of his six and a half seasons with the Bulls. But the versatile swingman also used

As one of the best rebounders of all time, Dennis Rodman was a valuable asset on both ends of the court.

his 6-foot-10 frame and court vision to average just under 5.0 rebounds and 5.0 assists per game with the Bulls.

Dennis Rodman was a unique personality on the Bulls' final three championship teams. Rodman was known for his brightly colored hair, his great ability to rebound the ball, and his defense. He had previously been on the Detroit Pistons, the team that had kept knocking the Bulls out of the playoffs. Rodman didn't score much, but he did lead the NBA in rebounding for seven straight years. That included his three seasons with the Bulls. He also won the Defensive Player of the Year award in back-to-back seasons before playing for the Bulls.

JORDAN'S JERSEY NUMBERS

Jordan's dominance made his retirement after 1993 a surprise. The Bulls retired his No. 23 while he was playing baseball in 1994. That meant he had to wear a different number when he came back to play for Chicago again in March 1995.

Jordan chose to wear No. 45 when he returned to the NBA. He had wanted to wear that number as a kid, but his older brother wore it. Jordan switched back to No. 23 for the 1995–96 season.

Jordan wore one other number with the Bulls. He had to wear a No. 12 uniform during a game in 1990. It's believed that his No. 23 jersey had been stolen and he did not have a personalized backup jersey. Because No. 12 was a generic team jersey, Jordan's name was not on the back.

CHAPTER 4

HIGHLIGHTS

Finally, after three seasons of losing to their rival Detroit Pistons in the playoffs, Chicago beat Detroit in the Eastern Conference Finals. The rivalry in both the 1991 regular season and the playoffs had been fierce. Fights had erupted in their games before. But now Detroit was on its way down, and Chicago was rising to the top of the league.

This was Jordan's and Chicago's first NBA Finals. Earvin "Magic" Johnson and the

Horace Grant slams it home against the Detroit Pistons.

Jordan holds the NBA Finals MVP trophy, a familiar sight in the 1990s.

Los Angeles Lakers were champions of the Western Conference. Johnson already had five rings and three MVPs to go along with his Hall-of-Fame career. There was plenty of star power on the court for the Finals. Los Angeles won a close Game 1, but the Bulls rebounded with four straight wins. After Scottie Pippen snagged a loose ball with six seconds left, the Bulls clinched the series. Jordan led the Bulls in scoring in the first four games. Pippen's 32 points led the way in Game 5. An emotional Jordan rested his head against the trophy he had chased for seven seasons. It was the beginning of a dynasty.

Jordan and the Bulls went on to win championships again in 1992 and 1993. While Jordan was the MVP in both of those Finals, other players had big roles. Pippen had 26 points in Game 6 in 1992 against Portland as Chicago clinched its second title. Guard John Paxson was the hero in Game 6 of the 1993 championship. Paxson hit a three-pointer with 3.9 seconds to play to give Chicago a 99–98 win over the Phoenix Suns. That helped the Bulls clinch their third championship in a row.

THE FIRST RETIREMENT

The Bulls were an impressive dynasty. They were also a dynasty that almost ended after three championships. Jordan retired after the 1993 season. He stepped away from the game of basketball to play a different sport. One of the greatest basketball players ever wanted to be a baseball player.

The announcement stunned the sports world. The Bulls had just won the 1992–93 NBA Finals. Jordan was still in the prime of

After a successful career in the NBA, Jordan retired from basketball to chase his dream of playing professional baseball.

his career. He had led the league in scoring for the seventh time that season.

The Bulls were still a great team without Jordan. But they weren't the best. Pippen tried to fill in for Jordan during his absence. The Bulls finished third in the Eastern Conference standings during the 1993–94 season. The New York Knicks

Michael Jordan's one season as a professional baseball player was with the Birmingham Barons. The Barons were a minor league team in the Chicago White Sox organization. He played 127 games during the 1994 season. He batted .202 with three home runs as an outfielder for the Barons. He also struck out 114 times in 436 at-bats.

ended Chicago's championship streak in the conference semifinals. The next year, the Bulls slipped to fifth place in the conference. But they got an unexpected boost when Jordan returned for the last 17 games of the 1994–95 regular season. He wasn't quite in peak basketball shape, however, and Chicago lost to the Orlando Magic in six games in the second round of the playoffs. Chicago's next season, however, would be a special one.

A SECOND THREE-PEAT

The Bulls set a slew of NBA records in the 1995–96 season. Chicago won 72 regular-season games. No team had previously won more games in a season.

The Bulls were simply dominant. They won by an average of more than 12 points per game. Chicago lost back-to-back games only once in the regular season. The Bulls went 15–3 in the playoffs as they won their fourth NBA championship. Their record of 72 wins stood until 2016 when the Golden State Warriors won 73 regular-season games.

Chicago capped its 72-win season with its fourth NBA championship in 1996. But the Bulls weren't done. They beat the Utah Jazz in back-to-back years for their fifth and sixth NBA Finals crowns.

Guard Steve Kerr provided the game-winning shot in 1997. He hit a big basket late in Game 6 to clinch a 90–86 win over Utah. The win also gave Chicago its fifth NBA title.

The final game of the NBA Finals in 1998 is perhaps one of the most memorable of Jordan's career. But Jordan made plenty more memories throughout his career. He won two Slam Dunk Contests. He played through the flu to score 38 points in Game 5 of the 1997 NBA Finals. A young Jordan scored 63 points against the Celtics in the 1986 playoffs. But no highlights were bigger than the six championships that he and the rest of the Bulls won during their dynasty.

CHAPTER 5

SECOND RETIREMENT

June 14, 1998, was the day Chicago beat Utah for its sixth NBA championship. It was also the last time Michael Jordan wore a Bulls uniform. It was the end of an era.

Jordan announced his second retirement in January 1999. The start of the season had been delayed by a labor dispute between players and team owners. When it was settled and the season was about to resume, Jordan said good-bye. His farewell from basketball made

After retiring and coming back, Jordan won a
fourth NBA Finals in 1996.

Jordan purchased the Charlotte Bobcats in 2010 and became managing partner of the franchise.

global headlines. Jordan thanked many people in his retirement statement, including his teammates, coaches, and fans around the world.

Some athletes have a hard time making ends meet once they retire. Jordan went the other way. He became a billionaire after his playing career ended. Nike pays him handsomely to use his name and image on its Air Jordan brand of shoes and clothing. Jordan's ownership of the Charlotte Hornets also had a positive impact on his bottom line.

After his retirement Jordan became part owner and president of basketball operations of the Washington Wizards. Jordan came out of retirement for the second time in his career in 2001. He joined the Wizards on the court for the 2001–02 season. He was 38 years old when he returned to play in the NBA. Jordan averaged 22.9 points per game that season. The next year he played in all 82 games and averaged an even 20.0 points per game. Then he walked away for good. Jordan was 40 years old when he played his last game on April 16, 2003.

But Jordan didn't stay away from the NBA after his final retirement as a player. He became a majority owner of the Charlotte Bobcats in 2010. As of 2018, he was the chairman of the renamed Charlotte Hornets.

Other players moved on from Chicago after 1998. Scottie Pippen joined the Houston Rockets the following season.

He later played four seasons with the Portland Trail Blazers. Pippen returned to Chicago for the 2003–04 season, his last year in the NBA.

JACKSON'S PATH

Phil Jackson also left the Bulls after the 1997–98 season. He returned to coaching in 1999 with the Los Angeles Lakers, and he picked up where he had left off with his new team. The Lakers and Jackson won five NBA titles between 1999 and 2010. His time in Los Angeles intersected with the prime of the careers of Kobe Bryant and Shaquille O'Neal, and he was able to get the most out of his talented but sometimes turbulent stars. Jackson finished his coaching career with 11 NBA championships. That's the most of any coach in NBA history.

After his coaching career was over in 2011, Jackson stayed in basketball. He joined the New York Knicks organization in 2014. Jackson was hired as the team's president of basketball operations.

HALL OF FAME

Jordan, Pippen, and Jackson were all inducted into the Basketball Hall of Fame. Jordan entered the Hall of Fame in

Michael Jordan's influence on Chicago can be seen outside United Center arena.

2009. Pippen joined Jordan in the Hall of Fame one year later. Jackson went in before both of his former players. His Hall of Fame induction took place in 2007. Former Bull Dennis Rodman

Jordan's famous No. 23 jersey was retired after his first retirement in 1994.

also was inducted in 2011. Rodman played three seasons with Chicago and won three NBA titles.

Jackson wasn't the only member of the Bulls dynasty who had later coaching success. Steve Kerr played for the Bulls from

1993 to 1998. He retired as a player in 2003. Kerr became the head coach of the Golden State Warriors in 2014. Stephen Curry and the Warriors won two championships in Kerr's first three seasons as head coach. And Kerr's Warriors broke the Bulls' single-season victory record when they went 73–9 in 2015–16.

The Bulls struggled after the dynasty came to an end. Chicago missed out on the playoffs for six straight years after winning the 1998 NBA Finals. Tim Floyd replaced Jackson as the head coach but lasted just four seasons. The Bulls won only 13 games during the 1998–99 season. Chicago hasn't made it back to the NBA Finals since the 1998 championship.

Jordan's impact on Chicago can be found in many places. Fans entering the United Center walk past a bronze statue of Jordan going airborne for a dunk. The Bulls retired Jordan's No. 23 jersey as well as No. 33 in honor of Pippen. Many NBA players such as LeBron James wear No. 23 in honor of Jordan. Chicago hasn't been the same since Jordan played his last game there. Michael Jordan and the Bulls will always be remembered as one of the greatest dynasties in NBA history.

CHICAGO BULLS

SPAN OF DYNASTY

- 1990–1998

NBA CHAMPIONSHIPS WON

- 6 (1991, 1992, 1993, 1996, 1997, 1998)

KEY STATS

- NBA record 72 wins in 1995–96
- 6–0 in NBA Finals series

KEY RIVALS

- Los Angeles Lakers, Detroit Pistons, New York Knicks

INDIVIDUAL AWARDS

NBA MVP AWARD

- Michael Jordan, 5 (1988, 1991, 1992, 1996, 1998)

FINALS MVP

- Michael Jordan, 6 (1991, 1992, 1993, 1996, 1997, 1998)

ALL-STAR MVP

- Michael Jordan, 3 (1988, 1996, 1998)
- Scottie Pippen, 1994

ROOKIE OF THE YEAR

- Michael Jordan, 1984–85

DEFENSIVE PLAYER OF THE YEAR

- Michael Jordan, 1987–88

COACH OF THE YEAR

- Phil Jackson, 1995–96

BASKETBALL HALL OF FAME MEMBERS

- Phil Jackson
- Michael Jordan
- Scottie Pippen
- Dennis Rodman

JUNE 19, 1984

The Chicago Bulls select Michael Jordan with the No. 3 overall pick in the NBA Draft.

OCTOBER 26, 1984

Michael Jordan makes his NBA debut with the Bulls.

JUNE 22, 1987

The Bulls acquire Scottie Pippen from the Seattle SuperSonics on the night of the NBA Draft.

JULY 10, 1989

The Bulls promote assistant coach Phil Jackson to head coach.

JUNE 12, 1991

Chicago defeats the Los Angeles Lakers in Game 5 of the NBA finals to win its first NBA championship.

JUNE 14, 1992

The Bulls beat the Portland Trail Blazers to win their second consecutive championship.

JUNE 20, 1993

Chicago completes its first three-peat by beating the Phoenix Suns in the NBA Finals.

OCTOBER 6, 1993

Jordan announces his surprising retirement from basketball in order to play professional baseball.

MARCH 18, 1995

Jordan makes a two-word statement to announce he's returning to the NBA, simply saying "I'm back."

JUNE 14, 1998

Jordan hits the game-winning shot to give the Bulls their sixth NBA title in his last game with Chicago.

GLOSSARY

BUZZER-BEATER
A shot that is made just before the shot clock or game clock expires.

CROSSOVER
A type of dribble in which a player quickly switches the ball from one hand to the other while dribbling.

DOUBLE-DOUBLE
Accumulating 10 or more of two certain statistics in a game.

DRAFT
A system that allows teams to acquire new players coming into a league.

DYNASTY
A team that has an extended period of success, usually winning multiple championships in the process.

FRANCHISE
A sports organization, including the top-level team and all minor league affiliates.

PLAYOFFS
A set of games played after the regular season that decides which team is the champion.

QUARTER
One of four 12-minute periods in an NBA game.

THREE-PEAT
When a sports team wins three championships in a row.

THREE-POINTER
Any shot taken behind the three-point line.

ONLINE RESOURCES

To learn more about Michael Jordan and the Chicago Bulls, visit abdobooklinks.com. These links are routinely monitored and updated to provide the most current information available.

BOOKS

Ervin, Phil. *Total Basketball*. Minneapolis: Abdo, 2016.

Graves, Will. *Basketball Record Breakers*. Minneapolis: Abdo, 2017.

Howell, Brian. *LeBron James vs. Michael Jordan*. Minneapolis: Abdo, 2018.

INDEX

ABOUT THE AUTHOR

Tyler Mason studied journalism at the University of Wisconsin–Madison. He has covered professional and college sports in Minneapolis and St. Paul, Minnesota, since 2009. He currently lives in Hudson, Wisconsin, with his wife.